Learning in Motion

Teaching Language Arts and Math through Movement

Second Grade

by Mary Murray

Carson-Dellosa Publishing Company, Inc.
Greensboro, North Carolina

Credits

Editor: Matthew Fisher

Layout Design: Van Harris

Inside Illustrations: Joe Eckstein

Cover Design: Peggy Jackson and Van Harris

Photo Credit: © Royalty-Free/Corbis

This book has been correlated to state, national, and Canadian provincial standards. Visit *www.carsondellosa.com* to search for and view its correlations to your standards.

ISBN 978-1-60022-229-0

Table of Contents

Language Arts Activities

Reading

Writing

Speaking and Listening

Math Activities

Number Sense

Measurement

Geometry

Algebra

Data Analysis and Probability

Introduction

Teachers have a wonderful opportunity to help students maintain physical wellness. *Learning in Motion* is packed with fun and challenging language arts and math activities that keep students out of their chairs and in motion. Students will experience and benefit from the connection between physical activity, good health, and improved learning. *Learning in Motion* engages students in a wide range of movement experiences, including stretching, ball handling, balancing, gymnastics, aerobics, strengthening exercises, and noncompetitive games.

You will find that these age-appropriate activities are quick and easy to incorporate into your daily schedule and curriculum. Many of the activities should be implemented in a large, open area, such as a gymnasium, the school cafeteria, or outdoors. Activities can also be conducted in a classroom; simply move aside tables or desks to create an open space for movement. Always remember to make safety a priority. Be mindful of student movement and the placement of equipment and materials while conducting these activities.

There is no need to worry about obtaining expensive sports equipment for these activities. *Learning in Motion* suggests materials that are inexpensive and readily available to teachers. In addition, a list on page 7 describes how to create your own materials for most of the activities. Some of the sports equipment used in this book, such as basketballs, softballs, sponge balls, footballs, beanbags, jump ropes, and plastic hoops, may be available from your school's physical education department. Most physical education teachers will be happy to let you borrow equipment when they learn that you are incorporating movement activities into your daily classroom routine!

Families are another great resource for donated materials. When you ask students' families for materials, you will often receive more than enough of the items that you request. Copy the letter on page 8 to send home with students. Remember to add any additional materials your class may need to the list.

So, get ready to move! You'll be amazed at the level of students' engagement as they begin *Learning in Motion*!

The Elements of Fitness

The three elements of fitness are **endurance, strength**, and **flexibility**. Each element is an important part of total fitness.

Endurance is a person's ability to repeat physical movement without becoming tired. It is developed by regularly participating in physical activities that raise heart rate. Physical activities that build endurance also strengthen cardiac and skeletal muscles. Examples of these activities are biking, jogging or running, walking fast, skating, swimming, and playing fast-paced sports, such as basketball and soccer.

Strength is the ability of a person's muscles to exert forces that can move parts of the body or other objects. Strength is developed through physical activities, such as climbing, toning exercises, sit-ups, push-ups, or weight-lifting. The more that muscles are used, the stronger they will become.

Flexibility is the ability to bend and move easily. When a person is flexible, his muscles and joints are able to move and bend with ease through a full range of motion. The more a person moves his joints and muscles, the more flexible he will become.

Fundamental Movement Skills

It is important that young children develop fundamental movement skills. Children who develop these skills early in life will be more active and have better coordination as they grow older. The activities in this book will help students develop these skills while also increasing their knowledge of language arts and math concepts.

Locomotor skills use larger muscles of the body and are characterized by movement of the entire body. Types of movement that build locomotor skills include hopping, crawling, running, and leaping.

Nonlocomotor skills are characterized by movements that are performed in a stationary position. Types of movement that build nonlocomotor skills include pushing, pulling, stretching, and balancing.

Manipulative skills are characterized by movements that control objects with the hands or feet. Types of movement that build manipulative skills include catching, throwing, kicking, and volleying balls.

Helpful Hints for Creating Materials

You may often find yourself without enough sports equipment for all of your students. The following list describes alternative ways to make some types of sports equipment.

- Team T-shirts: Keep several dark and light oversized T-shirts in the classroom. Many activities in this book require students to be divided into two groups. If needed, students can wear oversized T-shirts on top of their clothes to distinguish between the groups.

- Knotted towels: Tie a knot in the center of a hand towel, rag, or larger piece of fabric or felt.

- Towel-tube footballs: Push a hand towel through a cardboard paper towel tube so that the towel hangs from both ends of the tube. When throwing towel tubes, students should only hold the cardboard tubes. They should not grab or toss by the towels, as this will cause towels to pull out of the tubes after several tosses.

- Newspaper or tissue paper balls: Crumple a large sheet of newspaper or tissue paper into a tight ball.

- Sock balls: Roll one or two socks into a ball. Then, tuck the ball inside the opening of one sock to form a rounded ball.

- Paddles: For activities in which students volley balloons or newspaper and tissue paper balls, you can use plastic ice cream bucket lids as paddles. Or, you can create paddles by stretching a nylon stocking over a wire hanger that has been bent into a rounded shape. Cover any sharp edges of the hanger with duct tape.

- Traffic cones: Colorful beanbags or strips of fabric can be used to mark goals, bases, and starting and finishing lines.

- Carpet squares: Most carpet stores have plenty to give away or will sell them to teachers cheaply. You can also substitute old towels.

- Clipboards: Use a large, hardcover book with a clasping clothespin.

Dear Families,

Our class is incorporating physical activities into our daily lesson plans this year. These games and activities will help your children improve their math and language arts skills while encouraging them to remain physically fit. Some of the activities require specific materials that you may have at home. If you have any of the following items, we would be happy to accept donations. Or, if you would like to purchase an item and donate it to our classroom as a gift, we would greatly appreciate that as well.

- clean socks (old and mismatched are OK)
- paper towel, toilet paper, or wrapping paper cardboard tubes
- dark or light oversized T-shirts
- plastic ice cream buckets and lids
- old kitchen or bathroom hand towels
- old bathroom or beach towels
- colorful fabric and felt
- shoe boxes
- balloons
- carpet squares
- beanbags
- crepe paper
- sidewalk chalk
- sponge balls
- building blocks

- buckets
- newspaper and tissue paper
- wire hangers
- large, plastic hoops
- nonelastic string
- yarn
- various sizes of scoops and spoons
- various sizes of plastic containers
- jump ropes
- small baskets
- laundry baskets
- sports balls (baseballs, softballs, soccer balls, volleyballs, basketballs, etc.)
- CDs and cassettes with dancing or relaxing music

Sincerely,

Reference Tic-Tac-Toe

Students will identify the purposes of various reference materials in a game of tic-tac-toe.

Skill: Identifying purposes of reference materials

Setting: Outdoor blacktop area

Materials

- sidewalk chalk
- a variety of reference materials (dictionary, cookbook, phone book, newspaper, encyclopedia, atlas, almanac, gardening book, etc.)

Teacher Preparation:

1. Draw a large tic-tac-toe grid on blacktop with sidewalk chalk. Each space in the grid should be large enough for a student to stand in. Create several grids so that several groups can play at the same time.
2. Prepare a list of questions pertaining to the reference materials you have. For example, you can ask, "Where can I find a recipe for apple pie?" "How can I read more about my favorite sports athlete?" and "Where do I look to find the weather forecast for the week?"
3. Display the reference materials in a location where all of the students will see them.

Directions:

1. Divide students into two groups. Instruct both groups to stand around the perimeter of the game grid.
2. Explain that each student in one group should march in place. Each student in the other group should balance on one foot.
3. Choose which group will go first. Instruct groups to begin marching or balancing on one foot.
4. Read a question aloud from your list.
5. Ask a student from the first group to stand in a grid space and answer the question. If she answers correctly, she may stay in that space. If she answers incorrectly, a student from the other group may attempt to answer the question. If he is correct, he may take her place on the grid.
6. Read a question aloud for the second group. Continue asking questions with groups taking turns to answer.
7. Students standing in and around the grid should continue marching or balancing throughout the activity.
8. The round is over when three members from one group are standing in a row on the grid.
9. Repeat the activity until students identify each reference material several times.

Go Alphabetize!

Students will review how to alphabetize to the second letter in this game of dodgeball.

Skill: Alphabetizing to the second letter

Setting: Large, open indoor area

Teacher Preparation:

1. Print each of the letters *A*, *G*, *P*, and *Z* on separate sheets of paper.
2. Tape the letters along the length of a wall, in alphabetical order from left to right. Leave at least 10' (3 m) of space between each letter.
3. Copy the Go Alphabetize! Word Cards (page 11). Cut apart the cards. Or, write each word on a separate sheet of paper or card stock.
4. Place the word cards into the basket. Place the basket on the floor, close to the wall with the letters.
5. Create a center line by placing several traffic cones across the middle of the room. This line should be perpendicular to the wall with the letters.
6. Place half of the sponge balls on each side of the playing area.

Materials

- Go Alphabetize! Word Cards (page 11)
- 10–20 sponge balls
- black permanent marker
- paper or card stock
- basket
- traffic cones
- whistle

Directions:

1. Review with students how to alphabetize words to the second letter.
2. Divide students into two groups. Ask each group to spread out across a different half of the playing area. Explain that each group must stay on their half of the playing area.
3. When you blow the whistle, students in each group should pick up the balls on their side of the room and throw them at the students in the other group. Remind students to throw balls below the waist.
4. When a ball hits a student, he is out. The student who threw the ball should shout, "Go alphabetize!"
5. When a student catches a ball that is thrown at him, the student who threw the ball is out. The student who caught the ball should shout, "Go alphabetize!"
6. When a student is out, she should go to the wall with the letters and pick a word card from the basket. Then, she should sit along the wall in the place where her word would be alphabetized. Remind students to use the letters on the wall as an alphabetizing guide.
7. The game is over when all of the students in one group are out. The remaining students should each choose a word card and find the correct place to sit in the alphabetized row of words.

Extra Fun:

Arrange students in pairs. Give each pair a copy of the Go Alphabetize! Word Cards. Instruct partners to cut apart the cards and work together to place them in alphabetical order.

Go Alphabetize! Word Cards

act	lake	snake
apple	look	stars
ball	mighty	tent
brush	money	tunnel
doll	open	water
draw	orange	what
fish	penguin	yard
frog	please	yes
hand	rabbit	zebra
house	rope	zoo

Dictionary Madness

Students will use dictionaries to find the definitions of words and also perform different exercises and balances.

Skill: Using a dictionary

Setting: Classroom

Teacher Preparation:

1. Print one word from your current unit of study on each index card. Combine the word cards into one stack.
2. Copy the Movement Cards (pages 13–15). Make enough cards so that each student will have either one Movement Card or one dictionary.
3. Place the dictionaries and Movement Cards in an alternating pattern in a large circle on the floor. Make the circle large enough for students to march around it. Place a floor mat with each card that displays a movement requiring students to lay on the floor, such as sit-ups, tripod, and side leg-lifts.
4. Add the stack of word cards to the circle. Place a Movement Card with the stack of word cards.

Materials

- 10 student dictionaries
- 20 index cards
- Movement Cards (pages 13–15)
- floor mats or carpet squares
- black permanent marker
- CD or cassette player with music

Directions:

1. Instruct students to form a circle around the objects on the floor.
2. Explain that when you start the music, students should march in a line around the circle. When you stop the music, students should stop marching and turn to face the center of the circle.
3. The student closest to the stack of word cards should pick up the top card, say the word aloud, and then hold the card so that his classmates can see the word.
4. Students who stop in front of dictionaries should sit and use the dictionaries to find the definition of the word on the displayed card. When a student locates the definition in a dictionary, she should stand back up and march in place while she waits for the rest of her classmates to find the definition.
5. Each student who stops in front of a Movement Card should perform the movement on her card until all of the students with dictionaries are standing. The student in front of the stack of word cards should also perform the movement shown on the Movement Card in front of him.
6. When all of the students with dictionaries are marching in place, ask them to stop marching and to read the definition aloud in unison. Students performing movements should also stop and listen.
7. Students should then place the dictionaries back in the circle. When you start the music again, students should resume marching around the circle.
8. Continue the activity until each student has found several definitions and performed several movements.

Movement Cards

sit-ups

airplane balance

arm circles

jumping jacks

Movement Cards (continued)

tripod

side leg-lifts

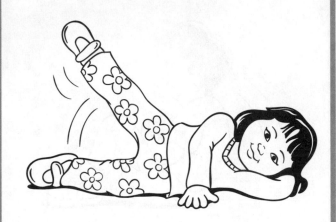

v-stand

jog in place

Movement Cards (continued)

balance on one foot

crab stand

toe touches

jump up and down

Tossing for Causes

Students will write cause-and-effect relationships, balance beanbags on their heads, and toss them into buckets.

Skill: Writing cause-and-effect relationships
Setting: Large, open area

Teacher Preparation:

1. Print the numbers 1 through 8 on separate index cards. Tape one card to the front of each bucket.
2. Copy the Cause Cards (page 17). Cut apart the cards.
3. Place one Cause Card in each bucket.
4. Place the buckets around the perimeter of the playing area.
5. Use masking tape to mark a tossing line in front of each bucket. Vary the distance between each line and its bucket.
6. Make one copy of the What Is the Effect? reproducible (page 18) for each student.

Materials

- Cause Cards (page 17)
- What Is the Effect? reproducible (page 18)
- beanbags
- 8 buckets or boxes
- 8 index cards
- clipboards
- pencils
- masking tape (or sidewalk chalk if outdoors)

Directions:

1. Provide each student with a What Is the Effect? reproducible, a pencil, and a beanbag. Students should attach their sheets to their clipboards.
2. Explain that each student should balance her beanbag on her head as she walks around the playing area. When she arrives at a bucket, she should toss her beanbag into the bucket as she stands on the tossing line. Each student may try three times to get a beanbag into a bucket before she must move to the next bucket.
3. When a student tosses a beanbag into a bucket, he should pick up the Cause Card inside the bucket and read it. Then, he should write an appropriate effect in the corresponding numbered space on his sheet. Remind students to place the Cause Cards back into the buckets when they are done.
4. Students should continue balancing their beanbags on their heads and tossing them into each bucket until they have written an effect for each cause.

Cause Cards

1. If you do not brush your teeth,

2. If you eat fruits and vegetables every day,

3. If you do not put your toys away,

4. If you help your family with chores,

5. If you do not wear a helmet while riding your bike,

6. If you break the rules during your soccer game,

7. If you finish your homework every night,

8. If you share with your friends,

What Is the Effect?

Directions: When you toss a beanbag into a bucket, pick up the Cause Card inside and read it. Then, write the effect in the correct space below. Remember to place the Cause Card back into the bucket after you have read it.

1. Effect: _____

_____

2. Effect: _____

_____

3. Effect: _____

_____

4. Effect: _____

_____

5. Effect: _____

_____

6. Effect: _____

_____

7. Effect: _____

_____

8. Effect: _____

_____

Pitch Long and Short

Students will identify long and short vowel sounds in this pitching activity.

Skill: Identifying long and short vowel sounds

Setting: Large, open area

Directions:

1. Review with students how to identify long and short vowel sounds.
2. Arrange students into groups of three.
3. Explain that one student in each group is a "pitcher." The other students are "catchers." One catcher in each group should stand approximately 3' (91 cm) from the pitcher. The other catcher should stand approximately 10' (3 m) from the pitcher.
4. Recite a word from the Long and Short Vowels reproducible (page 20). If a word has a long vowel sound, each pitcher should throw the ball to the farther catcher. If a word has a short vowel sound, each pitcher should throw the ball to the closer catcher.
5. After each throw, catchers should throw the balls back to the pitchers.
6. Continue reading words aloud. After 10 words, ask students to switch roles within their groups.

Materials
- sponge balls
- Long and Short Vowels reproducible (page 20)

Extra Fun:

Give each student a copy of the Long and Short Vowel reproducible. Instruct students to identify the vowel sound in each word by writing *long* or *short* on the lines provided.

Answer Key:

1. tree (long)
2. bed (short)
3. fat (short)
4. cane (long)
5. box (short)
6. book (short)
7. bump (short)
8. boat (long)
9. tin (short)
10. find (long)

11. eel (long)
12. egg (short)
13. ant (short)
14. aim (long)
15. add (short)
16. true (long)
17. up (short)
18. ice (long)
19. sick (short)
20. ate (long)

21. hot (short)
22. horse (short)
23. bat (short)
24. bake (long)
25. bell (short)
26. me (long)
27. plum (short)
28. bike (long)
29. milk (short)
30. rock (short)

Long and Short Vowels

Directions: Read each word below. If a word has a long vowel sound, write *long* in the blank. If a word has a short vowel sound, write *short* in the blank.

1. tree _____

2. bed _____

3. fat _____

4. cane _____

5. box _____

6. book _____

7. bump _____

8. boat _____

9. tin _____

10. find _____

11. eel _____

12. egg _____

13. ant _____

14. aim _____

15. add _____

16. true _____

17. up _____

18. ice _____

19. sick _____

20. ate _____

21. hot _____

22. horse _____

23. bat _____

24. bake _____

25. bell _____

26. me _____

27. plum _____

28. bike _____

29. milk _____

30. rock _____

Synonym Skipping

Students will identify synonyms for words and skip around the room.

Skill: Identifying synonyms

Setting: Large, open indoor area

Teacher Preparation:

1. Make one copy of the Synonym Game Grid (page 23) for each student.
2. Place one plastic hoop for each student on the floor around the center of the room.
3. Place a pencil inside each hoop.

Materials

- Synonym Sentences List (page 22)
- Synonym Game Grid (page 23)
- large plastic hoops or large sheets of construction paper
- pencils

Directions:

1. Review with students that synonyms are words that have similar meanings.
2. Give each student a copy of the Synonym Game Grid. Instruct students to stand around the perimeter of the room.
3. Explain that students will skip in one direction around the room. As they skip, lead students in singing the following song to the tune of "Jingle Bells."

    Synonyms, synonyms, words that mean the same.
    Synonyms, synonyms, we can play the game, hey!
    We'll skip around the room and take a little hike,
    We'll find two special words whose meanings are alike.

4. When students finish the song, they should skip to the hoops in the center of the room and listen as you recite an instruction.
5. Start with the first sentence from the Synonym Sentences List (page 22). Call out, "Write the number *1* in the box that contains the synonym for *small*." Then, recite the sentence, "The girl picked up a very *small* leaf." Students should write the number *1* in the square with the synonym *tiny*.
6. When each student completes the instruction, she should stand and balance on one foot in her hoop. When all of the students are balancing, ask one student to call out the correct answer. Allow students who answer incorrectly to try again.
7. Instruct students to return to the perimeter of the room and resume skipping and singing. Remind students to take their game grids but to leave the pencils in the hoops.
8. Continue the activity until students complete their game grids.

Synonym Sentences List

1. The girl picked up a very **small** leaf. (tiny)

2. "I left your jacket in the **automobile**," said Mom. (car)

3. Jason was **angry** because his sister spilled juice on his new shirt. (mad)

4. Mom baked **delicious** cookies. (tasty)

5. He read the **final** page of the book. (last)

6. Marissa's brother offered to **throw** the ball with her so that she could practice. (toss)

7. She wore a sweatshirt that was too **large**. (big)

8. Coach Marx had a big **grin** on his face when he saw Jenna score a goal. (smile)

9. Jessica wanted to **begin** piano lessons. (start)

10. My grandfather was very **cheerful** when we came to visit. (happy)

11. The teacher asked us to **create** animals from modeling clay. (make)

12. **Several** people wore shirts with our school's name on them. (many)

13. Jillian gave Mr. Murray a **gift** for his birthday. (present)

14. Isaiah tried to **block** the goal. (stop)

15. The dog pushed the ball **beneath** the couch. (under)

16. Ms. Garvey swatted the **insect** with a flyswatter. (bug)

17. Micah likes to **gather** rocks and keep them in a box. (collect)

18. When her brother went away to summer camp, Betty was **upset**. (sad)

19. Lori had to **leap** over the puddle on the sidewalk. (jump)

20. When the big storm arrived, it became very **breezy**. (windy)

Synonym Game Grid

Directions: Your teacher will read a word and a sentence aloud. Find the word on the grid that is a synonym for a word in the sentence. Write the number that your teacher announces in the blank.

bug _____	car _____	big _____	tiny _____
start _____	windy _____	happy _____	mad _____
make _____	under _____	last _____	many _____
sad _____	toss _____	stop _____	present _____
tasty _____	collect _____	jump _____	smile _____

Antonym Bounce

Students will name antonyms and dribble basketballs.

Skill: Naming antonyms

Setting: Large, open indoor area

Teacher Preparation:

1. Write each antonym from the list below on a separate index card.
2. Glue each index card to a sheet of construction paper for increased visibility.
3. Tape the cards to the floor randomly around the center of the room. Leave at least 10' (3 m) between each card.

Materials

- basketballs or playground balls
- 18 index cards
- 18 sheets of construction paper
- black permanent marker
- whistle
- transparent tape

Antonyms:

hot, first, slow, sleep, dark, day, boy, float, empty, tall, high, work, stop, near, open, good, loud, over

Directions:

1. Review with students that antonyms are words that are opposites of each other. Explain that there are Antonym Cards placed around the room, and that each one has a word printed on it.
2. Give each student a ball. Instruct students to stand around the perimeter of the room. Allow students to practice dribbling while standing in place.
3. Instruct students to practice dribbling the balls while walking around the perimeter of the room.
4. Blow the whistle to signal students to dribble their balls toward the center of the room, find partners, and move to the nearest word cards. Instruct students to stop dribbling the balls when they find word cards.
5. Call on one pair of students at a time. One student should read the word, and then her partner should name an antonym of that word.
6. Instruct students to return to the perimeter of the room and continue dribbling the balls. Repeat the activity until each student has a chance to name an antonym.
7. Encourage students to find different partners and Antonym Cards for each round.

Toss and Tell

Students will describe characters in stories as they toss beanbags back and forth.

Skill: Describing characters in books

Setting: Large, open indoor area

Teacher Preparation:

1. Create Character Cards by printing a different book title and a character name from that book on each index card. If possible, copy a picture of each character and affix the pictures to the cards.
2. Tape the Character Cards to the floor or walls randomly around the room.
3. Display the books at the front of the room.

Materials

- beanbags
- index cards
- storybooks
- transparent tape
- black permanent marker
- whistle

Directions:

1. Review with students how to describe a book's characters by how the characters look, act, and speak. Review the main characters from each of the books displayed at the front of the room.
2. Arrange students in pairs. Give each pair a beanbag. Ask partners to stand approximately 5' (1.5 m) apart, near a Character Card.
3. Explain that partners should toss a beanbag back and forth and think about the character on the Character Card they chose to stand near.
4. When you blow the whistle, students should stop tossing the beanbags.
5. Call on one pair of students at a time. The student in that pair that is holding the beanbag should call out a sentence that describes how the character on her card looks, acts, or speaks.
6. When each student holding a beanbag has described a character, ask each pair to move to a new Character Card.
7. Continue the activity until each student describes several characters.

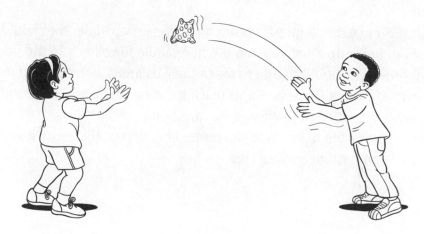

Balloon Batting

Students will enhance their reading comprehension skills as they volley balloons through the air.

Skill: Identifying and answering reading comprehension questions

Setting: Large, open area

Teacher Preparation:

1. Copy the Question Cards (page 27). Make one copy for every three students.
2. Create a paddle for each student by taping a different Question Card to each side of each ice cream bucket lid or paddle.
3. Prepare a list of *who, what, where, when, why,* and *how* questions about a book your class has read recently. For example, questions about *Goldilocks and the Three Bears* might include, "Why did the bears go for a walk?" "Who entered the bears' house?" and "What piece of furniture did Goldilocks break?"
4. Mark a starting line at one end of the playing area and a center line in the middle of the area with traffic cones.
5. Inflate and tie one balloon for each student. Inflate several extra balloons to replace those that may pop during the activity. Place the balloons along the length of the center line. Caution: Before completing this activity, ask families about possible latex allergies. Also, remember that uninflated or popped balloons may present a choking hazard.

Materials

- balloons
- Question Cards (page 27)
- traffic cones
- plastic ice cream bucket lids or paddles
- transparent tape

Directions:

1. Instruct students to stand along the starting line.
2. Give each student a paddle. Ask students to read the words on each side of their paddles.
3. Stand at the opposite end of the playing area. Explain that students should listen carefully as you ask a question aloud.
4. If the type of question matches a question card on a student's paddle, she should hop to the center line. Then, she should pick up a balloon and use her paddle to volley it to the side of the area where you are standing. Students should try not to touch their balloons with their hands as they volley them.
5. When students with matching Question Cards reach the area where you are standing, ask the question again. Invite one student to answer the question.
6. Instruct students to return the balloons to the center line. Repeat the activity until several examples of each type of question have been answered.

Question Cards

Who?	What?
Where?	When?
Why?	How?

Sentence Shooters

Students will differentiate between fragments and complete sentences as they shoot basketballs.

Skill: Differentiating between fragments and complete sentences

Setting: Large, open area

Teacher Preparation:

1. Place the laundry baskets along one side of the playing area. Leave approximately 15' (4.6 m) of space between each basket.
2. Use masking tape to mark a shooting line approximately 10' (3 m) in front of each basket.
3. Make six copies of the Basketball Shot Sentences and Fragments reproducible (page 29). Attach each sheet to a clipboard.
4. Place a clipboard and a pencil approximately 25' (7.6 m) behind each shooting line.

Materials

- Basketball Shot Sentences and Fragments reproducible (page 29)
- 6 basketballs or playground balls
- 6 laundry baskets
- 6 sharpened pencils
- 6 clipboards
- masking tape (or sidewalk chalk if outdoors)

Directions:

1. Review with students the difference between a sentence fragment and a complete sentence.
2. Divide students into six groups. Instruct each group to form a line behind a different shooting line.
3. Group members will take turns shooting balls toward the baskets. If a student misses the basket, he should retrieve the ball and pass it to the next student in his line. If a student shoots a ball into a basket, she should jog to her group's clipboard.
4. The student should choose a sentence from the sheet and decide whether it is complete or incomplete. If the sentence is complete, she should write the letter *S* in the space provided. If the sentence is a fragment, she should write the letter *F* in the space provided. The student should then jog to the end of her group's line.
5. Continue the activity until each group's Basketball Shot Sentences and Fragments sheet is complete.

Answer Key:

1. F	5. S	9. F	13. F
2. F	6. F	10. F	14. S
3. S	7. F	11. S	15. F
4. F	8. S	12. F	16. S

Basketball Shot Sentences and Fragments

Directions: Decide if each sentence below is a complete sentence or a fragment. In each blank, write the letter *S* for a complete sentence or the letter *F* for a fragment.

1. _____ I will find

2. _____ Jason came to my

3. _____ Marcia and Sara are good friends.

4. _____ He let the

5. _____ Josh is not playing soccer this year.

6. _____ Mr. Wilson was about to

7. _____ Our family took

8. _____ It was the best vacation ever.

9. _____ We went to the Rocky Mountains in

10. _____ School is the only

11. _____ You can play if you would like.

12. _____ I am glad you are

13. _____ He is the only person who

14. _____ Josiah walked the dog to the park.

15. _____ Clarissa and Julie

16. _____ Jackson took the puppy home for a walk.

Dancing for Details

Students will write detail sentences that support topic sentences as they dance around the room.

Skill: Creating complete paragraphs

Setting: Large, open indoor area

Teacher Preparation:

1. Copy the Topic Sentence Cards (page 31). Cut apart the cards.
2. Glue each topic sentence to a larger piece of construction paper for increased visibility.
3. Place the plastic hoops randomly around the center of the room.
4. Place a Topic Sentence Card, several sheets of lined paper, and a pencil inside each hoop.

Materials

- Topic Sentence Cards (page 31)
- 16 large plastic hoops
- 3' (91 cm) segments of colorful ribbon or crepe paper
- construction paper
- lined paper
- pencils
- CD or cassette player with dancing music
- whistle

Directions:

1. Review with students how every paragraph should have a main idea and several details. Remind them that the main idea always comes first, and that the details give more information about the main idea.
2. Give each student a segment of ribbon. When you start the music, students should dance around the perimeter of the room, holding their ribbons above their heads so that the ribbons fly through the air as they move.
3. When you blow the whistle, students should form a group of three around each plastic hoop.
4. One student in each group should read the topic sentence aloud. Each group should then work together to write three detail sentences that support their topic sentence.
5. When each group finishes writing three detail sentences, they should jump into the air and wave their ribbons. Walk to each of these groups. Group members should give you their sheet of paper, then return to the perimeter of the room and resume dancing.
6. Repeat the activity until each student has written detail sentences for several topic sentences. Encourage students to gather at different hoops with different classmates for each round.

Variation:

After each round, ask groups to read their paragraphs aloud to the class. After each group reads their paragraph, classmates can applaud by jumping and waving their ribbons in the air.

Topic Sentence Cards

Dogs are great pets.	You should always wear a seat belt in a car.
Saving money is important.	It is fun to play a team sport.
Soccer is a great sport.	Exercise is important for good health.
I love riding my bike.	The sun is important for life on Earth.
A watermelon is an interesting fruit.	Planting a garden is a fun family activity.
You have to practice to be a good basketball player.	Many animals live near ponds.
I enjoy listening to music.	Parties are fun.
Orange juice is delicious.	Students should always do their homework.

Go Balance!

Students will use adjectives in written and spoken sentences as their partners perform balancing activities.

Skill: Using adjectives

Setting: Large, open indoor area

Teacher Preparation:

1. Make one copy of the Balancing Sentences reproducible (page 33) for each group of four students.
2. Make one copy of the Go Balance! Cards (page 34) for each group. Cut apart the cards.

Materials

- Balancing Sentences reproducible (page 33)
- Go Balance! Cards (page 34)
- pencils

Directions:

1. Arrange students into groups of four.
2. Provide each group with a copy of the Balancing Sentences reproducible and a set of Go Balance! Cards.
3. Choose one student in each group to be the group leader. Each leader should shuffle his group's balance cards, then turn over the top card.
4. When each group leader says, "Go balance!" students in her group should balance in the position shown on the top card.
5. Each leader should read aloud the first sentence from the Balancing Sentences reproducible. Then, he should rewrite the sentence in the space provided, adding several adjectives to make the sentence more detailed and interesting. His group members should maintain their balancing position while the leader writes his new sentence and reads it aloud.
6. Repeat the activity several times. Choose a new leader for each group and instruct students to turn over a new balance card for each round.

Balancing Sentences

Directions: Choose a sentence to read aloud. After you read it aloud, rewrite the sentence, adding adjectives to make the sentence more interesting. Then, read your new sentence aloud to your group.

1. The mouse ate cheese.

   _____

2. The man ate lunch.

   _____

3. The woman carried a bag.

   _____

4. The bear smelled the food.

   _____

5. The girl walked home.

   _____

6. The boy went to the school.

   _____

7. The cat ran away.

   _____

8. The man rode to the game.

   _____

Go Balance! Cards

crab kick

airplane balance

v-stand

pointer stand

Jump, Sit, and Describe

Students will use adverbs in sentences as they jump around in a large circle with classmates.

Skill: Using adverbs

Setting: Large, open indoor area

Materials
- large index cards
- black permanent marker
- whistle

Teacher Preparation:

1. Write each of the sentences from the list below on a separate index card. You can use several of the sentences more than once. You will need one card for each student.
2. Tape the index cards to the floor in a large circle. Leave approximately 2' (61 cm) of space between each card.

Directions:

1. Review with students that adverbs are words that describe verbs. Explain that adverbs often end with the suffix -ly.
2. Instruct students to form a circle around the cards. Each student should stand in front of a card.
3. Explain that each time you blow the whistle, students should jump in the same direction around the circle to the next card.
4. After students have jumped several times, call out, "Sit and describe!" Each student should then stop jumping and sit in front of the nearest card.
5. Invite one student to read her sentence aloud as it is written on the card. She should then read her sentence a second time, adding an adverb to make the sentence more interesting.
6. After several students have added adverbs to their sentences, instruct students to stand and re-form the circle.
7. Continue the activity until each student has several opportunities to use adverbs in sentences.

Sentence List:

1. The turtle crawled.
2. He ran to the store.
3. She fixed the bike.
4. My mom sang.
5. Tony walked.
6. The flower grew.
7. Joe painted.
8. Marcie jogged home.
9. Dad slept.
10. Jessie played.
11. Uncle Mike worked.
12. The clouds moved.
13. The sun shone.
14. It rained.
15. The dog barked.
16. The wind blew.
17. Kelly stepped on the rock.
18. Mary whispered.
19. Sophie kicked the ball.
20. Joe rang the bell.

Letter Hop and Skip

Students will identify parts of letters and addressed envelopes as they hop and skip on one foot across the room.

Skill: Identifying parts of letters and envelopes
Setting: Large, open indoor area

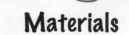

Materials

- 8 sheets of chart paper
- black permanent marker
- masking tape

Teacher Preparation:

1. Write different informal letters on four sheets of chart paper. Include the following components in each letter: date, greeting, body, closing, and signature.
2. Draw a large envelope on each of the remaining sheets of chart paper. Address the envelopes so that each envelope matches one letter. Include the following components on each envelope: address, return address, and stamp.
3. Tape matching letters and envelopes next to each other on a wall, with approximately 10' (3 m) of space between each pair.
4. Use masking tape to mark a starting line 20' (6.1 m) from each set of chart papers on the wall.

Directions:

1. Review with students the different parts of letters and envelopes.
2. Divide students into four groups. Ask each group to form a line behind a different starting line.
3. When you call out, "Hop to the (part of a letter or envelope)," the first student in each line should hop on one foot toward that line's pair of chart papers and point to the designated part of the letter or envelope.
4. When each student identifies the correct part, instruct her to skip to the end of her group's line.
5. Continue naming different parts of letters and envelopes until each student has several opportunities to identify named parts.

October 1
Dear Mom,
Thank you for helping me with my homework.
Love,
Amy

Soccer Goal

Students will correct misspelled words and dribble soccer balls.

Skill: Spelling

Setting: Large, open area

Teacher Preparation:

1. Copy the Soccer Spelling List (page 38). In the left column, write misspelled words from your current unit of study.
2. Make one copy of the list of misspelled words for each pair of students.
3. Attach each list to a clipboard.
4. Place a soccer ball, a clipboard with a spelling list, and a pencil for each pair of students at one end of the playing area.
5. Use traffic cones to mark a starting line at one end of the playing area.
6. Place four traffic cones in a straight line at the other end of the playing area, leaving 10' (3 m) of space between each cone.

Materials

- Soccer Spelling List (page 38)
- soccer balls
- pencils
- traffic cones
- clipboards

Directions:

1. Arrange students in pairs. Ask each pair to stand near a set of materials.
2. Instruct students to review the list of misspelled words.
3. When you call out, "Ready, set, dribble!" one student in each pair should dribble a soccer ball across the playing area, around a cone, and back toward the starting line.
4. When a student returns to the starting line, he should write the correct spelling of one word on his pair's spelling list.
5. The second student in each pair should then dribble the ball around a cone and back again.
6. When the student returns, she should write the correct spelling of another word on the list.
7. Continue the activity until each pair spells all of the words on their list correctly.

Soccer Spelling List

Directions: Write the correct spelling of each misspelled word in the second column.

1. _____   _____

2. _____   _____

3. _____   _____

4. _____   _____

5. _____   _____

6. _____   _____

7. _____   _____

8. _____   _____

9. _____   _____

10. _____   _____

11. _____   _____

12. _____   _____

Toss It!

Students will read passages aloud and toss foam footballs back and forth with partners.

Skill: Developing read-aloud skills

Setting: Large, open area

Teacher Preparation:

1. Make one copy of the Toss It! Story Cards (pages 40–42) for each pair of students. Cut apart the cards.
2. Place each set of cards in a separate envelope.

Directions:

1. Arrange students in pairs.
2. Give each pair of students an envelope of story cards and a foam football.
3. Explain that partners should stand approximately 5' (1.5 m) apart and toss their ball back and forth to each other. Each time both partners toss and catch the ball, they should take one giant step backward before tossing the ball again.
4. When one of the student's in the pair misses a catch, each partner should choose a card from their envelope and read it quietly.
5. Each partner should then read his story card aloud with fluency and expression.
6. When partners finish reading, they should return to tossing the football, starting approximately 5' (1.5 m) apart. Continue the activity until each pair reads all of their passages.

Variation:

Conduct this activity as a group. Instruct students to form a large circle, face the center, and toss a football to each other. If a student drops or misses the ball, the student who threw the ball should choose a card and read it aloud.

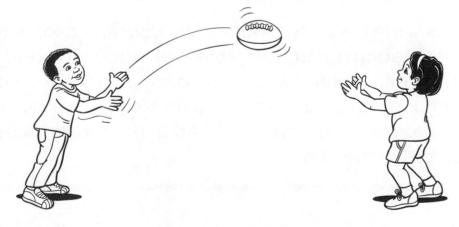

Toss It! Story Cards

Bob and Judy were ready to plant their garden. Judy was in charge of flower seeds. Bob was in charge of vegetable seeds. They each brought their own shovel for digging. Bob's mom let them use her watering can to water the seeds. Bob and Judy felt great when they finished. They could hardly wait to watch their garden grow.

Our trip to the pond was fun. Jason caught a frog. It jumped out of his hands three times! I found some great rocks for my rock collection. Diane picked up a bundle of sticks. She plans to glue them together to make a small raft. We skipped stones and ate the snacks that Mom packed for us. It was a great way to spend a Saturday morning.

It was the best game that Marie had ever played. Jim passed her the ball and Marie dribbled it toward the goal. She kicked it into the net, over the goalie's head. The goalie was surprised! He had never seen someone so quick! The coach ran onto the field and picked up Marie. The entire team gathered around her, shouting and jumping. It was the best game ever!

Art class is the best. My teacher, Mrs. Jones, is a lot of fun. She really enjoys teaching art. Last week, we made clay pots. Now, we are painting with watercolors. I am painting a picture of a sunset. I think it will look great. Jennifer liked making rubber stamps. That was fun! I use my stamp every day. Art is my favorite class. I think I will be an artist when I grow up.

Toss It! Story Cards (continued)

Jason got a skateboard for his birthday. He loves his new skateboard. Every day, he rides to the park. Jason likes riding down hills with the wind blowing against him. He feels like a bird when he rides his skateboard. "It is just like flying," Jason always tells his friends.

We have a chore list at our house. When I was younger, I had simple jobs, like picking up toys. My chores are harder now. Yesterday, I had to fold and put away all of the laundry. Today, I have to sweep the garage. Tomorrow, I will vacuum the car. I know it is important to have chores. We need to share the work. But, I wish I could be young again so that I could have easier jobs.

Washing dishes with my family can be great fun. Mom clears the table. Dad fills the sink with soapy water. I love it when he puts soap bubbles on his face. He pretends that he has a white beard. Andy and I dry the dishes and put them away. Sometimes, we sing our favorite songs while we wash the dishes. Washing the dishes does not take a long time when we work together.

The bus ride to school usually takes 20 minutes. We get on the bus at 7:25 A.M. We arrive at school by 7:45 A.M. David likes to sit in the back with his friends. I sit in the front with my friends. I like riding the bus, except in the winter. It is very cold outside. We have to wait a long time at the bus stop. We are very excited when the bus arrives on those days!

Toss It! Story Cards (continued)

Our guinea pig, Ted, is like a member of our family. He squeals when we sit down for dinner because he wants to eat, too! Now, we always give him a carrot before we eat. Ted watches movies with us on family night. We even take him outside when we do yard work. He loves to eat the grass. Ted's favorite place to go is Grandma and Grandpa's house. He loves the attention they give him.

The Fox family went to the park to have a picnic. Mom packed the sandwiches, chips, and cookies. Joe put the sodas into a cooler with ice. Carrie grabbed a softball and a bat. Dad carried the dog to the car. They spent the afternoon at the park. Dad told funny stories. Mom surprised them with a special dessert. Everyone had a great time.

Dear Justin,

I am having a great time at the water park. You would love it here. We spent three hours on the bumper boats and waterfalls last night. Today, I am going to go on every slide at least five times! Our room is really nice. It is decorated like a log cabin. This is the best water park! I wish you were here.

Your friend, Max

Dear Grandpa,

Florida is great! It is 90 degrees today. We swam in the Gulf of Mexico. The sand on the beach is bright white! Dad said we are going sailing tomorrow. I can't wait! We ate at some really good restaurants, too. I hope you are having a great week. I miss you.

Love, June

Volley and Follow

Students will follow two-step directions and volley balls against a wall.

Skill: Following two-step directions

Setting: Large, open indoor area

Teacher Preparation:

1. Copy the Directions Cards (pages 44–45). You will need one card for each student. Cut apart the cards.
2. Glue each Directions Card to a larger piece of construction paper for increased visibility.
3. Tape the cards to the walls around the perimeter of the room. Leave 15' (4.6 m) of space between each card.

Materials

- volleyballs
- Directions Cards (pages 44–45)
- colorful construction paper

Directions:

1. Give each student a volleyball. Instruct each student to stand near a Directions Card.
2. Explain that students should volley the balls against a wall.
3. When a student misses a ball, he should read the card he is standing near and follow the directions on the card.
4. When a student has completed his two-step directions, he can move to any open Direction Card in the room.
5. Continue the activity until each student follows several sets of two-step directions.

Directions Cards

Perform 10 jumping jacks, then 15 sit-ups.	Jog in place to the count of 30, then perform 10 push-ups.
Perform five wall push-ups, then 10 leg-lifts.	Crab walk in a large circle, then perform a crab stand to the count of 20.
Jog across the room, then spider walk back.	Perform 12 push-ups, then 12 squats.
Perform 10 arm circles, then balance on one foot to the count of 20.	Perform 12 sit-ups, then 12 wall push-ups.
Perform 15 toe touches, then 15 jumping jacks.	Spider walk across the room, then crab walk back.

Directions Cards (continued)

March in place to the count of 20, then perform 10 wall push-ups.	Perform 10 toe touches, then 20 arm circles.
Perform 20 forward arm circles, then 20 backward arm circles.	Jog across the room, then spider walk back.
Perform 10 leg-lifts, then 10 wall push-ups.	Jog in place to the count of 30, then balance on one foot to the count of 10.
Hop on one foot in a large circle, then balance on one foot to the count of 20.	Jump up and down 15 times, then perform 15 sit-ups.
Hop across the room, then perform a crab walk back.	Balance on one foot to the count of 20, then perform 10 push-ups.

Kick It and Write It

Students will read and write numerals to 1,000 as they kick crumpled paper balls around the room.

Skill: Reading and writing numbers to 1,000
Setting: Large, open indoor area

Materials

- Number Word Cards (page 47)
- colorful paper
- write-on/wipe-away board and markers (or chart paper and markers)
- whistle

Teacher Preparation:

1. Copy the Number Word Cards (page 47). Cut apart the cards.
2. Glue each Number Word Card to a small piece of colorful paper. Allow the glue to dry completely.
3. Crumple each sheet of paper into a ball.

Directions:

1. Divide students into four groups. Assign each group a name (Red Group, Green Group, etc.).
2. Give each student a ball of colorful paper. Explain that students should dribble their paper balls like soccer balls around the room.
3. Explain that when you blow the whistle, you will name one group. The students in that group should stop and uncrumple their balls of paper. The students in the other groups should continue dribbling their paper balls.
4. Instruct the students in the named group to read the Number Word Cards, then write the numerals represented by the number words on the board.
5. When each student finishes writing, instruct students to re-crumple their paper balls and toss them to classmates so that each student has a new ball to kick.
6. Continue the activity until each student reads and writes several different numerals on the board.

Number Word Cards

eight hundred twelve	six hundred ninety-three	two hundred forty-seven	fifty-four	three hundred nine
sixty-five	thirty-eight	seven hundred sixty	one hundred forty-nine	three hundred sixty
one thousand	seven hundred twenty	nine hundred ninety-nine	one hundred seventy-eight	eight hundred sixteen
fourteen	ninety-seven	eighteen	nineteen	two hundred twenty-two
four hundred seventy-seven	nine hundred forty-two	twenty-nine	eighty-one	seventy-three

Dribble and Order

Students will order numbers as they dribble basketballs across the room.

Skill: Ordering numbers to 1,000

Setting: Large, open indoor area

Teacher Preparation:

1. Write each number from the Number Ordering reproducible (page 49) on a separate index card.
2. Divide the cards into three piles. Place each pile into a basket.
3. Mark a starting line at one end of the room with traffic cones.
4. Place the baskets along the wall opposite the starting line.

Materials

- Number Ordering reproducible (page 49)
- basketballs
- 50 index cards
- 3 small baskets
- black permanent marker
- pencils
- traffic cones

Directions:

1. Arrange students into groups of three. Ask each group to form a line behind the starting line.
2. Explain that the first student in each group should dribble a basketball across the room, choose a card from one of the baskets, and dribble the ball back to the starting line.
3. When a group member returns with the ball, the next student in her group should also dribble the ball across the room and choose a card.
4. When a group has five cards, group members should sit and arrange their number cards in order from least to greatest.
5. When each group finishes and you have checked the order of their cards, they should return the cards to a basket.
6. Repeat the activity several times. Or, instruct students to order the cards from greatest to least or group the cards by even and odd numbers.

Extra Fun:

Give each student a copy of the Number Ordering reproducible to complete.

Answer Key:

1. 21; 97; 191; 263; 974
2. 39; 70; 189; 448; 671
3. 20; 99; 103; 360; 856
4. 1; 88; 290; 404; 1,000
5. 12; 67; 581; 956; 999
6. 2; 75; 299; 341; 641
7. 49; 211; 721; 882; 1,000
8. 33; 221; 559; 654; 987
9. 19; 188; 200; 434; 999
10. 28; 99; 499; 797; 1,000

Number Ordering

Directions: Write each set of numbers in order from least to greatest.

1. 97; 263; 191; 974; 21 _____

2. 671; 448; 39; 70; 189 _____

3. 20; 856; 99; 103; 360 _____

4. 404; 290; 88; 1; 1,000 _____

5. 956; 581; 67; 12; 999 _____

6. 341; 641; 75; 299; 2 _____

7. 721; 1,000; 49; 211; 882 _____

8. 559; 987; 654; 221; 33 _____

9. 188; 19; 200; 999; 434 _____

10. 1,000; 499; 28; 99; 797 _____

Even and Odd Jump

Students will practice identifying even and odd numbers as they jump rope and perform different tasks.

Skill: Identifying even and odd numbers
Setting: Large, open indoor area

Materials

- Even and Odd Task Cards (pages 51–52)
- Even and Odd Recording Chart (page 53)
- jump ropes
- construction paper
- pencils

Teacher Preparation:

1. Copy the Even and Odd Task Cards (pages 51–52). Cut apart the cards.
2. Glue each task card to a larger piece of construction paper for increased visibility.
3. Tape the task cards to the walls around the perimeter of the room. Leave approximately 15' (4.6 m) of space between each card.
4. Make one copy of the Even and Odd Recording Chart (page 53) for each pair of students.

Directions:

1. Arrange students in pairs. Provide each pair with an Even and Odd Recording Chart and a pencil.
2. Instruct each pair to stand in front of a task card. Give each pair a jump rope.
3. Explain that each partner will take a turn jumping rope. The partner not jumping should count the number of times she can jump in a row.
4. When a student misses a jump, she should record the number of jumps she made in a row on her recording sheet. She should also write whether it is an even or odd number.
5. If a student jumped an even number of times, she should complete an even task. If she jumped an odd number of times, she should complete an odd task.
6. When a student finishes a task, her partner should take a turn jumping rope and performing a task.
7. When a pair finishes, they may move to any open Even and Odd Task Card.

Even and Odd Task Cards

Even	Odd
Perform 10 jumping jacks.	Perform 15 jumping jacks.

Even	Odd
Spin the jump rope in a circle on the floor 4 times.	Spin the jump rope in a circle on the floor 7 times.

Even	Odd
Perform 12 sit-ups.	Perform 17 sit-ups.

Even	Odd
Use the jump rope to make a shape with 4 sides.	Use the jump rope to make a shape with 3 sides.

Even	Odd
Perform an airplane balance to the count of 20.	Perform an airplane balance to the count of 25.

Even	Odd
Wiggle the jump rope on the floor like a snake to the count of 10.	Wiggle the jump rope on the floor like a snake to the count of 3.

Even and Odd Task Cards (continued)

Even	Odd
Perform a crab stand to the count of 20.	Perform a crab stand to the count of 23.

Even	Odd
Use the jump rope to make a shape with 6 sides.	Use the jump rope to make a shape with 5 sides.

Even	Odd
Jog in place to the count of 30.	Jog in place to the count of 35.

Even	Odd
Perform 10 jumping jacks and 10 wall push-ups.	Perform 15 jumping jacks and 15 wall push-ups.

Even	Odd
Perform 20 forward arm circles.	Perform 25 backward arm circles.

Even	Odd
Balance on one foot to the count of 20.	Balance on one foot to the count of 17.

Even and Odd Recording Chart

Name: _____		Name: _____	
Number of Times Jumped	Even or Odd?	Number of Times Jumped	Even or Odd?

Addition Pass

Two teams of students will try to intercept a ball before the opposing team scores a point in this mental math addition game.

Skill: Addition

Setting: Large, open indoor area

Teacher Preparation:

Mark a center line by placing several traffic cones across the center of the playing area.

Materials

- sponge ball
- 2 large plastic hoops
- traffic cones
- black permanent marker
- write-on/wipe-away board and markers (or chart paper and markers)

Directions:

1. Divide students into two groups. Each group should stand on a different side of the playing area.

2. Choose two students from each group to be "goalkeepers." Each pair of goalkeepers should hold a plastic hoop waist high at the far end of their group's side of the playing area.

3. Instruct each group to spread out on their side of the playing area. Explain that students are not allowed to move from their place while the ball is being passed. They may only rotate by pivoting on one foot. Demonstrate how to pivot by keeping one foot stationary while you turn your body with your other foot.

4. Write an addition equation on the board so that students can see it.

5. Instruct students to use mental math to find the sum. Then, ask one student to call out the answer.

6. Choose which team will get the ball first. This team should try to pass the ball the number of times designated by the sum of the equation before throwing the ball through their plastic hoop.

7. Give the ball to a student on the starting team. If the team successfully passes the ball the correct number of times and makes a shot, the other team should perform the number of jumping jacks designated by the sum of the equation.

8. If the ball is dropped while being passed or if a student throws the ball to the hoop and misses, the other team may try to pass and score a goal.

9. Repeat the activity, displaying a new equation for students to solve. Teams should take turns starting each round.

Row and Solve

Students will solve addition and subtraction facts as they move and stretch in this rowing activity.

Skill: Addition and subtraction

Setting: Large, open area

Teacher Preparation:

1. Print a number with one, two, or three digits on each index card.
2. Place the sheets of construction paper on the floor or ground randomly around the area. Leave approximately 10' (3 m) of space between each sheet.
3. Place three number cards facedown on each sheet of construction paper.
4. Tie a knot in the middle of each hand towel.
5. Place a sheet of lined paper, a pencil, and a knotted hand towel next to each sheet of construction paper.

Materials

- hand towels
- 45 index cards
- 15 sheets of colorful construction paper
- black permanent marker
- lined paper
- pencils
- CD or cassette player with music
- clipboards if outdoors

Directions:

1. Arrange students in pairs. Instruct each pair to sit next to a sheet of construction paper.
2. Demonstrate how students should use the hand towels. Partners in each pair should "row" by spreading their legs wide, placing the bottoms of their feet together with their partner's feet, and holding opposite ends of the hand towel.
3. Explain that when you start the music, students should begin pulling on the hand towels, back and forth between partners, in a rowing motion. Remind students to hold their ends of the hand towels securely, as letting go suddenly may cause their partner to fall backward.
4. After a few minutes, stop the music. Each partner should stop and turn over one number card.
5. One partner in each pair should record an addition or subtraction problem on the lined paper using the numbers on their upturned cards.
6. The other partner in each pair should then solve the written problem.
7. When their math fact is complete, each pair of students should resume rowing until you check all of the equations.
8. Instruct students to turn their cards facedown and move to new sheets of construction paper. Each pair should take their lined paper with them. Remind students to leave the pencils and hand towels at each station.

Mental Math Bounce

Students will perform mental addition to find the sums as they improve their ball-handling skills.

Skill: Using mental math
Setting: Large, open area

Teacher Preparation:

1. Prepare a list of addition equations from your current unit of study. Write one equation for each student.
2. Print the sum of each equation on a separate index card.

Materials

- playground ball
- index cards
- black permanent marker

Directions:

1. Review with students how to use mental math to solve addition problems.
2. Ask students to form a circle around you. Give each student one index card with a sum printed on it.
3. Explain that you will call out an addition equation from your list. Students should use mental math to solve the equation.
4. After you call out the equation, bounce the ball high into the air. The student with the sum of the designated equation on her index card should run to catch the ball. Her classmates should scatter around the playing area.
5. When the student catches the ball, she should call out the answer to the equation and the phrase, "Mental math!" All of the students should then freeze.
6. The student holding the ball should throw it to a classmate. Students should continue passing the ball the number of times designated by the sum of the equation. The last student to catch the ball should then dribble it toward you.
7. Take the ball and instruct students to re-form a circle around you. Repeat the activity until each student has a chance to answer an equation using mental math.

Variation:

Create a list of subtraction equations and a set of index cards with the correct differences. Repeat the activity by asking students to use mental math to find the differences.

Multiplication Relay

Students will solve multiplication equations as they run a relay race.

Skill: Multiplication

Setting: Large, open indoor area

Teacher Preparation:

1. Create multiplication "batons" by printing a simple multiplication equation onto each cardboard tube.
2. Place a sheet of chart paper and several markers on the floor in each corner of the room.

Materials

- 4 sheets of chart paper
- 15 cardboard toilet paper tubes
- colorful markers
- black permanent marker

Directions:

1. Divide students into four groups. Instruct each group to form a line in a different corner of the room.
2. Give each of the first two students in each line a multiplication baton.
3. Explain that each student with a baton should read the multiplication equation on her baton and run to the next corner.
4. When a student with a baton arrives at the next corner, she should record her baton's equation on the chart paper placed there, then pass the baton to the first student in that corner's line.
5. The student who passed the baton should then record the answer to her equation, sign her name, and move to the end of the line in that corner. The student who received the baton should run to the next corner.
6. Continue the activity until each student has recorded answers to several equations. After several rounds, introduce batons with new multiplication equations into the activity.

© Carson-Dellosa

Fraction Bowling

Students will identify and name fractions in this bowling activity.

Skill: Identifying and naming fractions

Setting: Large, open indoor area

Teacher Preparation:

1. Copy the Fraction Cards (pages 59–60). Cut apart the cards.
2. Write the correct fraction name on the back of each card.
3. Use transparent tape to affix each fraction card to a shoe box. Tape the cards so that students can flip them to check the answers. When each box is placed on its side, the fraction card should be visible on top.
4. Place the boxes against the walls around the perimeter of the room. The opening of each box should face away from the wall.
5. Use masking tape to mark a bowling line approximately 10' (3 m) in front of each box.

Materials

- Fraction Cards (pages 59–60)
- 18 shoe boxes without lids
- softballs
- masking tape
- transparent tape

Directions:

1. Review with students how to name fractions.
2. Give each student a softball.
3. Explain that students should walk around the room, bowling softballs into different shoe boxes.
4. When a student successfully bowls his ball into a box, he should walk to the box and recite the name of the fraction shown on top. Remind students that they should turn the cards over to check their answers.
5. Continue the activity until each student recites all of the fraction names.

Answer Key:

Page 59: 1. $\frac{1}{6}$, 2. $\frac{4}{8}$, 3. $\frac{3}{4}$, 4. $\frac{2}{6}$, 5. $\frac{2}{4}$, 6. $\frac{3}{4}$, 7. $\frac{1}{8}$, 8. $\frac{2}{3}$, 9. $\frac{1}{4}$

Page 60: 10. $\frac{2}{3}$, 11. $\frac{6}{8}$, 12. $\frac{1}{2}$, 13. $\frac{1}{4}$, 14. $\frac{1}{2}$, 15. $\frac{1}{6}$, 16. $\frac{2}{8}$, 17. $\frac{3}{4}$, 18. $\frac{1}{3}$

Fraction Cards

1.	2.	3.
4.	5.	6.
7.	8.	9.

Fraction Cards (continued)

10.
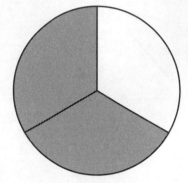

11.
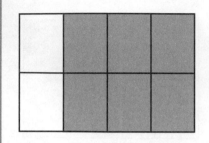

12.
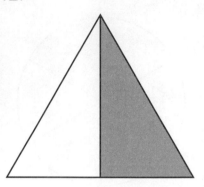

13.
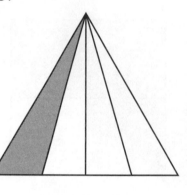

14.
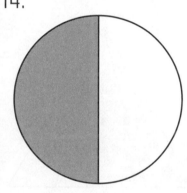

15.
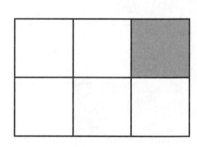

16.
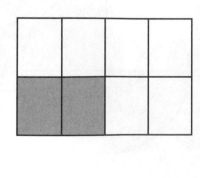

17.
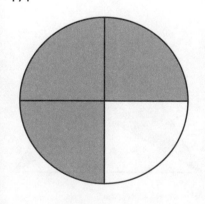

18.
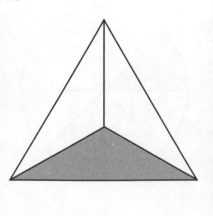

Learning in Motion • CD-104240

Reasonable Running

Students will identify reasonable estimates of measurement by performing various movements.

Skill: Identifying reasonable estimates

Setting: Large, open area

Directions:

1. Review with students how to identify reasonable and unreasonable estimates when measuring length, weight, and time.
2. Explain that you will read an estimate aloud. If students think it is a reasonable estimate, they should run to the other side of the room. If students think it is an unreasonable estimate, they should perform three push-ups.
3. Read each of the estimates below aloud and assess students' understanding of reasonable estimation.

Estimates:

Reasonable Estimates:

1. The length of his shoe is 10 inches.
2. It took 5 minutes for Megan to ride her bike around the block.
3. My teacher is 6 feet tall.
4. The elephant weighs 2,000 pounds.
5. Recess is 30 minutes long.
6. The bus ride to school is 30 minutes long.
7. The bag of apples weighs 3 pounds.
8. His bedroom doorway is 3 feet wide.
9. We drove 60 miles to Grandma's house. It took 1 hour.
10. Her pencil was 6 inches long.
11. The movie is 2 hours long.
12. The watermelon weighed 10 pounds.

Unreasonable Estimates:

1. The length of his shoe is 2 miles.
2. It took 5 hours for Megan to ride her bike around the block.
3. My teacher is 16 feet tall.
4. The elephant weighs 40 pounds.
5. Recess is 320 minutes long.
6. The bus ride to school is 24 hours long.
7. The bag of apples weighs 42 pounds.
8. His bedroom doorway is 59 feet wide.
9. We drove 60 miles to Grandma's house. It took 7 days.
10. Her pencil was 45 inches long.
11. The movie is 11 hours long.
12. The watermelon weighed 2 ounces.

Wheelbarrow Time

Students will practice telling time to the nearest quarter hour as they walk in the wheelbarrow position around the room.

Skill: Telling time to the nearest quarter hour

Setting: Large, open indoor space

Materials

- Analog Clock Face Cards (page 63)
- Digital Clock Face Cards (page 64)
- transparent tape

Teacher Preparation:

1. Copy the Analog and Digital Clock Face Cards (pages 63–64). Cut apart the cards.
2. Print a different time to the nearest quarter hour on each clock.
3. Print the correct time in words on the back of each card.
4. Tape the clock faces faceup to the floor around the perimeter of the room. Place the tape so that students can flip the cards to check their answers. Leave approximately 20' (6.1 m) of space between each Clock Face Card.

Directions:

1. Arrange students in pairs. Demonstrate how to walk in the wheelbarrow position. Ask a student to hold the ankles or shins of his partner as she walks on her hands around the room.
2. Explain that as pairs travel around the room, they will find Clock Face Cards taped to the floor. When a pair reaches a card, the "wheelbarrow" partner should read the time aloud.
3. The partner holding the wheelbarrow's ankles should use the time in a sentence, such as, "I am going to soccer practice at **9:15**."
4. After reading each card, partners should switch roles and move to the next card. Remind students to be courteous of classmates who may not travel as quickly around the room.

Analog Clock Face Cards

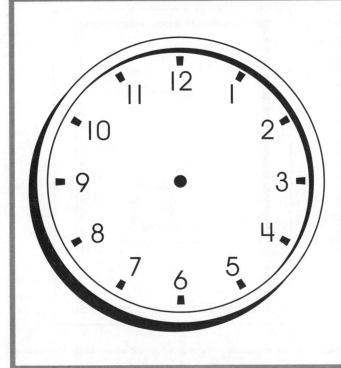
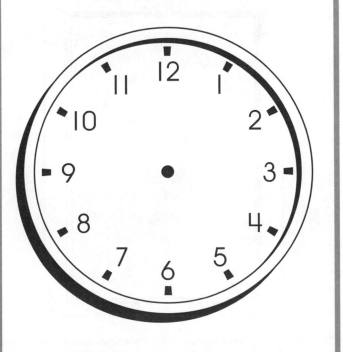

Digital Clock Face Cards

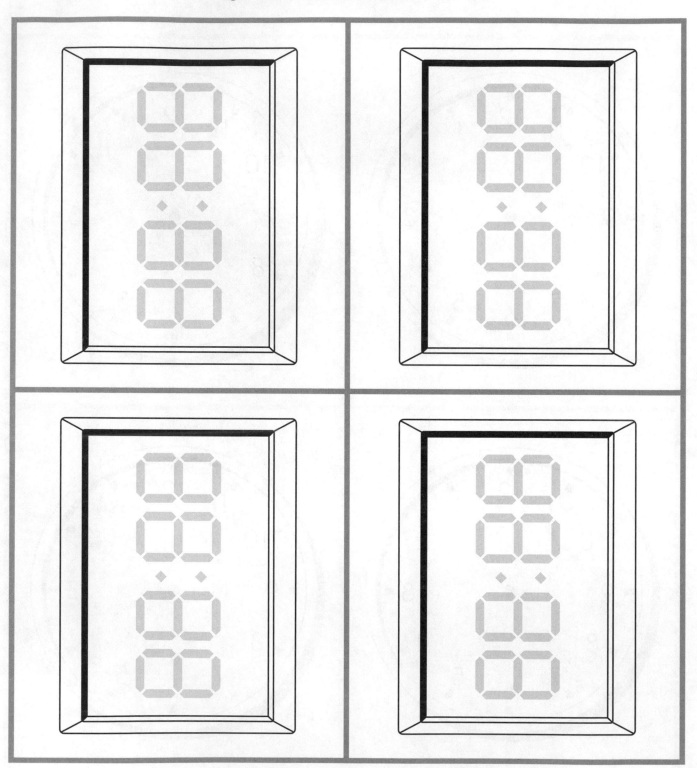

Learning in Motion • CD-104240

Hop Around the Clock

Students will determine intervals of time as they hop toward the center of the room.

Skill: Determining time intervals

Setting: Large, open area

Materials

- Time Interval Problems reproducible (page 66)

Directions:

1. Review with students how to determine time intervals.
2. Instruct students to stand in a large circle, facing the center of the room. Stand in the center of the circle.
3. Explain that you will read a problem from the Time Interval Problems reproducible (page 66) aloud. Students should perform mental math to find the time interval that the problem describes.
4. When you call out, "Time to hop!" each student should hop toward the center of the circle once for each hour of the time interval. For example, when you read the problem, "The class was at the park from 11:00 A.M. until 4:00 P.M. How many hours were they at the park?" each student should hop five times toward the center of the circle.
5. Ask one student to call out the correct answer.
6. Instruct students to hop back to their starting positions.
7. Repeat the activity for each time interval problem.

Extra Fun:

Give each student a copy of the Time Interval Problems reproducible to complete.

Answer Key:

1. 5 hours
2. 3 hours
3. 3 hours
4. 1 hour
5. 2 hours
6. 8 hours
7. 2 hours
8. 4 hours
9. 2 hours
10. 8 hours

Time Interval Problems

Directions: Read each time interval problem. Answer the questions on the lines provided.

1. _____ The class was at the park from 11:00 A.M. until 4:00 P.M. How many hours were they at the park?

2. _____ Jenny went shopping with her mom from 9 A.M. until 12 P.M. How many hours did they shop?

3. _____ Mark played at Zach's house from 8:00 until 11:00 in the morning. How many hours did Mark and Zach play?

4. _____ Mary helped her mother in the garden from 6:00 to 7:00 at night. How many hours did Mary help her mother?

5. _____ The movie played from 3:00 P.M. until 5:00 P.M. How many hours did the movie play?

6. _____ Naomi's birthday party will be held from 10:00 A.M. until 6:00 P.M. How many hours will Naomi's birthday party last?

7. _____ The school store is open between 11:00 A.M. and 1:00 P.M. How many hours is the school store open?

8. _____ Hot lunch is served from 10:00 A.M. until 2:00 P.M. How many hours is hot lunch served?

9. _____ Jake went to the store at 4:00 P.M. and came home at 6:00 P.M. How many hours was he gone?

10. _____ Alice goes to school from 8:00 in the morning until 4:00 in the afternoon. How many hours is Alice at school?

Centimeter March

Students will measure objects to the nearest centimeter as they march around in a circle.

Skill: Measuring objects to the nearest centimeter

Setting: Classroom

Teacher Preparation:

1. Provide an index card for each student and number them consecutively.
2. Arrange student desks in a large circle and place one numbered index card on each desk. Or, arrange the cards in a large circle on the floor.
3. Place a ruler and a common object with each numbered card.
4. Measure the length of each object to the nearest centimeter. Create an answer key by recording the lengths of the objects with the corresponding numbers from the index cards.

Materials

- rulers with centimeter markings
- common objects, such as pencils, pens, crayons, strings, blocks, books, etc.
- index cards
- black permanent marker

Directions:

1. Review with students how to measure an object's length to the nearest centimeter.
2. Instruct students to stand around the circle that you have prepared.
3. Explain that when you start the music, students should march around the circle of objects.
4. When you stop the music, each student should use a ruler to measure the object that is nearest to him.
5. Ask several students to call out the measurements of their objects. Check their answers with the answer key.
6. Start the music again and repeat the activity. Change the type of movement to skipping, hopping, crawling, or other movements for each round.

Long Jump Pop!

Students will compare the distances that classmates leap as they perform long jumps on bubble packaging material.

Skill: Comparing distances

Setting: Large, open indoor area

Teacher Preparation:

1. Use duct tape to secure one end of the bubble packaging material (bubble side up) to the floor.
2. Unroll the bubble packaging material and secure the other end of the roll to the floor with duct tape.
3. Place several small pieces of duct tape along the sides of the bubble packaging material to secure it to the floor.
4. Mark a starting line approximately 1' (30 cm) behind one end of the bubble packaging material.

Materials

- large roll of bubble packaging material
- duct tape
- black permanent marker
- spool of nonelastic string
- scissors

Directions:

1. Arrange students in pairs. Instruct pairs to form a line starting several feet behind one end of the bubble packaging material.
2. Explain that, one at a time, a student from each pair will leap as far as he can from a standing position onto the bubble packaging wrap. After he leaps, his partner should write his initials on his landing spot with a permanent marker.
3. The leaping student's partner should hold one end of the string at the starting point, while his partner unrolls the spool of string to his landing spot. Instruct the student to cut the string at the heel of his landing spot.
4. The pair should then move to the back of the line. The second student in the pair will have an opportunity to leap when the pair reaches the front of the line.
5. After each student has measured his leap, students in each pair should lay their strings on the floor to compare the lengths of their leaps.
6. Instruct students to find new partners to compare their lengths of string. Repeat until each student compares his string with several classmates.

Variation:

Use a long sheet of mural paper instead of bubble packaging material. Partners can trace outlines of the leaping students' footprints on the paper with the permanent marker.

Estimation Jump

Students will estimate volume as they gallop sideways and jump in and out of plastic hoops.

Skill: Estimating volume

Setting: Classroom

Teacher Preparation:

1. Create one measuring station on a desk or table for each pair of students, with approximately 10' (3 m) of space between each station. At each station, place one ice cream bucket filled with a material to measure, one empty plastic container, one scoop, and a pencil. Vary the size of the empty container and the scoop at each station.

2. Place a large plastic hoop on the floor at each station.

3. Make one copy of the Estimation Recording Chart (page 70) for each pair of students.

Materials

- plastic ice cream buckets
- materials to measure volume, such as sand, packing peanuts, uncooked rice, etc.
- various sizes of plastic containers
- various sizes of scoops or spoons
- large plastic hoops
- Estimation Recording Chart (page 70)
- pencils

Directions:

1. Arrange students in pairs. Give each pair a copy of the Estimation Recording Chart.

2. Explain that students will travel between each measuring station by performing a sideways gallop.

3. At each station, partners should look at the empty container and make an estimate of how many scoops or spoonfuls of the material in the ice cream bucket will fill it. Each pair should write their estimate in the Estimate of Volume column on their chart.

4. Then, each partner should jump in and out of the hoop the number of times designated by their estimate.

5. Partners should then work together to fill the empty container, counting the actual number of scoops needed to fill the container. Partners should write this number in the Actual Volume column on their chart.

6. Then, the pair of students should join hands to jump in and out of the hoop together. They should jump the same number of times as the number of scoops needed to fill the empty container.

7. Each pair should then empty the contents of the plastic container back into the ice cream bucket.

8. Repeat the activity by instructing pairs to gallop sideways to a different set of materials for each round. Remind students to leave the pencils at the measuring stations.

Estimation Recording Chart

Station	Estimate of Volume	Actual Volume
1		
2		
3		
4		
5		
6		
7		
8		
9		
10		
11		
12		
13		
14		
15		

Congruency Course

Students will identify congruent shapes as they improve their balance and strength by traveling along an obstacle course.

Skill: Identifying congruent shapes

Setting: Classroom

Teacher Preparation:

Materials
- card stock
- 10 large plastic hoops
- masking tape
- 3 shoe boxes
- 10' (3 m) length of yarn
- 2 chairs
- table

1. Cut six different polygons (triangle, square, pentagon, hexagon, octagon, trapezoid, etc.) from card stock. Create at least one shape for each student in addition to two of each shape to place in the room.
2. Create an obstacle course in a line perpendicular to one wall of the room. Follow these steps to set up an obstacle course, or design your own.
   a. Arrange the plastic hoops into five rows of two.
   b. Create a balancing line by affixing a 5' (1.5 m) length of masking tape to the floor.
   c. Arrange the shoe boxes in a line with 3' (91 cm) of space between each box.
   d. Place the table after the boxes.
   e. Place the two chairs 3' (91 cm) apart. Tie each end of the yarn to a chair, approximately 2' (61 cm) above the ground.
3. Place one of each shape at a different place in the obstacle course, such as after the hoops, at the end of the balancing line, at the end of the shoe boxes, etc.
4. Tape one of each shape along the wall at the end of the course, with 10' (3 m) of space between each shape.

Directions:

1. Review with students that congruent shapes are two polygons that have the same shape and size.
2. Give each student a shape. Instruct students to form a line at the beginning of the obstacle course.
3. Explain that students should travel along the obstacle course by stepping inside each hoop, walking heel-to-toe along the balance line, jumping over the shoe boxes, crawling underneath the table, then rolling on the floor between the chairs and underneath the line of yarn.
4. Students should hold their shapes as they travel along the course. When students come to each shape displayed along the course, they should check to see whether their shapes are congruent. When a student finds a shape along the course that is congruent to her own, she should call out, "Congruent!"
5. When each student finishes the course, she should sit below the shape on the wall that is congruent to her own.
6. Ask students to exchange shapes and repeat the obstacle course.

Hopscotch Symmetry

Students will identify symmetrical and asymmetrical shapes as they play this variation of hopscotch.

Skill: Identifying symmetrical and asymmetrical shapes

Setting: Large, open area

Teacher Preparation:

1. If your playground does not have pre-drawn hopscotch grids, use chalk to draw one grid for each group of four students on a blacktop or sidewalk area. To conduct this activity indoors, use masking tape to create hopscotch grids on the floor.
2. Cut symmetrical and asymmetrical shapes from card stock. Each shape should be approximately 3" (7.6 cm) in size. Create one shape for each hopscotch grid square.
3. Place a shape in the upper left corner of each hopscotch grid square so that students will not step on or slip on a shape.
4. Place a basket next to the beginning of each hopscotch grid.

Materials

- hopscotch grids
- beanbags
- small baskets
- card stock
- chalk (or masking tape if indoors)

Directions:

1. Arrange students into groups of four.
2. Explain that group members should take turns tossing a beanbag onto their grid, then hopping with one foot in each square to the space where the beanbag landed.
3. When a student reaches a beanbag, he should pick up the shape in that square, describe it, and tell whether the shape is symmetrical or asymmetrical.
4. The student should then pick up the beanbag, hop to the end of the grid, and hop back to the beginning of the grid. When a student reaches the beginning of the grid, he should place his shape in his group's basket.
5. The next student in line should then take a turn. Remind students to aim for squares that still have paper shapes. If a student misses a square with a shape, she should try again. Each group should play until all of the shapes in their grid have been picked up and placed in the basket.
6. When each group finishes, group members should create one pile of symmetrical shapes and one pile of asymmetrical shapes.
7. Then, instruct each group to replace the shapes on their grid, switch hopscotch grids, and repeat the activity.

Soccer Dribble

Students will find the missing parts of several addition and subtraction equations after dribbling soccer balls across a grassy playing area.

Skill: Finding missing parts of equations
Setting: Grassy outdoor area

Teacher Preparation:

1. Make one copy of the Number Equation Cards (page 74) on card stock for each group of four students. Cut apart the cards.
2. Write the correct missing part of the equation on the back of each card.
3. Mark a starting line along one side of a grassy area with several traffic cones.

Materials

- soccer balls
- Number Equation Cards (page 74)
- card stock
- traffic cones

Directions:

1. Arrange students into groups of four. Instruct each group to form a line behind the starting line.
2. Provide each group with a set of Number Equation Cards and a soccer ball.
3. The first student in each line should read the equation on a card and use mental math to find the missing number.
4. When the student has the answer, she should dribble the ball the number of times designated by the missing number. She should stop the ball by placing her toe on top of the ball. Then, she should turn and dribble the ball the same number of times back to the starting line. The other students in her group should count the number of times she dribbles aloud.
5. When a student returns to the starting line, she should call out the missing part of her equation. She should then turn over the card to check the answer.
6. The next student in line should then take the ball and continue the activity.
7. Continue the activity until each student has an opportunity to find several missing parts of equations.

Extra Fun:

Give each student a copy of the Number Equation Cards reproducible to complete.

Answer Key:

1. 4   3. 5   5. 3   7. 10   9. 4
2. 3   4. 16   6. 10   8. 8   10. 6

Number Equation Cards

1. $5 + \underline{\hspace{2cm}} = 9$	2. $\underline{\hspace{2cm}} + 6 = 9$
3. $10 - \underline{\hspace{2cm}} = 5$	4. $1 + \underline{\hspace{2cm}} = 17$
5. $\underline{\hspace{2cm}} + 7 = 10$	6. $20 - \underline{\hspace{2cm}} = 10$
7. $2 + \underline{\hspace{2cm}} = 12$	8. $8 + \underline{\hspace{2cm}} = 16$
9. $14 - \underline{\hspace{2cm}} = 10$	10. $\underline{\hspace{2cm}} + 4 = 10$

Scooting Addends

Students will name pairs of addends as they pull themselves around the room on carpet squares.

Skill: Naming pairs of addends

Setting: Uncarpeted, open indoor area

Teacher Preparation:

1. Print a two-digit number on each index card. Make at least one card for each student.
2. Place the cards faceup on the floor, spread randomly around the room.

Materials

- carpet squares
- index cards
- black permanent marker
- whistle

Directions:

1. Give each student a carpet square.
2. Instruct students to spread out across the room. Students should place their carpets squares facedown on the floor.
3. Demonstrate how students should move by kneeling on their carpet squares and pulling themselves with their hands.
4. Blow the whistle to signal that students should begin moving around the room on their carpet squares.
5. About 30 seconds later, blow the whistle a second time. Each student should place his hand on the number card nearest to him. More than one student may place a hand on a number card.
6. Call out a number on one of the cards. If a student is touching a card with the number that is called, he should name two pairs of addends whose sums are equal to the number called. If more than one student is touching the card, have each student name different addends for the number called.
7. Continue to call out numbers as students name pairs of addends.
8. Blow the whistle again, signaling students to resume moving. Continue the activity for several rounds, stopping every 30 seconds to call out new numbers.

Variation:

Instead of calling out a number, recite an addition or subtraction equation that corresponds to a number on a card. Students should use mental math to determine the sum or difference. If a student is touching the number card that represents the sum or difference, she should stand and jog in place.

Hoop Roll

Students will improve their understanding of probability by tossing beanbags onto grids of numbers after they roll hoops and jog across the room.

Skill: Probability

Setting: Large, open indoor area

Teacher Preparation:

Materials

- Probability Cards (page 77)
- 2 sheets of chart paper
- basket
- black permanent marker
- 4 large plastic hoops
- 4 beanbags
- traffic cones

1. Mark a starting line at one end of the playing area with traffic cones. Place the hoops along the starting line.
2. Mark a finish line with traffic cones at the opposite side of the area, approximately 20' (6.1 m) from the wall.
3. Create number grids by drawing a large tic-tac-toe grid on each sheet of chart paper.
4. Print one of the following numbers in each space of the first grid: 66, 6, 4, 7, 70, 53, 62, 12, 8. Print one of the following numbers in each space of the second grid: 59, 52, 49, 57, 8, 3, 51, 65, 54.
5. Copy the Probability Cards (page 77). Cut apart the cards and place them in the basket.
6. Place the beanbags and basket of Probability Cards on the floor behind the finish line.
7. Place each grid approximately 6' (1.8 m) past the finish line.

Directions:

1. Arrange students in pairs. Instruct pairs to form four lines behind the starting line.
2. One student in each pair will be a "roller" and the other student in each pair will be a "jogger."
3. Each roller should roll a hoop upright across the room toward the finish line. Joggers should jog alongside rollers to the finish line.
4. When each pair reaches the finish line, the jogger should pick a Probability Card from the basket and read it aloud.
5. Partners should determine which number grid has a better probability that a beanbag will land on the type of number described on the card.
6. Each jogger should stand on the finish line and toss a beanbag onto the chosen grid, aiming for a number that will fit the description on her pair's card.
7. Check the location of each pair's beanbag on the grid. Then, have students remove their beanbag from the grid and return the Probability Cards to the basket.
8. Partners should then switch roles. Each new roller should roll a hoop back to the starting line and give the hoop to the next pair in line.

Probability Cards

an even number	a number less than 15	a number between 50 and 60
an odd number	a two-digit number	a number between 4 and 10
a number greater than 6	a one-digit number	a number with 5 in the tens place

Sports Graphs

Students will record and graph data as they demonstrate their favorite sports.

Skill: Representing data

Setting: Large, open indoor area

Teacher Preparation:

1. Copy the Sports Tables and Sports Graph reproducibles (pages 79–80). Print the words *basketball*, *soccer*, and *four square* as the headings for each table.
2. Make one copy of the labeled Sports Tables and Sports Graph reproducibles for each student.
3. Print the words *basketball*, *soccer*, and *four square* on the board.

Materials

- Sports Tables and Sports Graph reproducibles (pages 79–80)
- basketballs
- soccer balls
- playground balls
- colorful pencils
- write-on/wipe-away board and markers (or chart paper and markers)

Directions:

1. Ask students to answer the following question: "Which game do you prefer to play, basketball, soccer, or four square?"
2. Each student that prefers to play four square should bounce a ball against a wall with her hand, let it bounce on the floor, and bounce it again on the wall. Allow students to continue this activity while you record their names on the board under the heading *four square*. When you have recorded all of the names, ask students to return to their seats.
3. Each student that prefers to play basketball should dribble a basketball while you record each student's name on the board under the heading *basketball*. Then, ask students to return to their seats.
4. Each student that prefers to play soccer should dribble a soccer ball around the playing area while you record each student's name on the board under the heading *soccer*. Then, ask students to return to their seats.
5. Lead students in a discussion as they analyze the data by counting and comparing how many students prefer each sport.
6. Then, instruct students to record the data on their own Sports Tables and Sports Graph. Students should complete the name and tally charts first, then create bar graphs using the data.

Variation:

Make blank copies of the Sports Tables and Sports Graph reproducibles for each student. Repeat the activity by using other types of sports or activities.

Learning in Motion • CD-104240

Sports Tables

Name Chart: Write the names of students under the type of activity they prefer in the chart below.

Tally Chart: Make tally marks to count how many students prefer each type of activity in the chart below.

Name _____ Date _____

Sports Graph

Directions: Create a bar graph with the data that you collected.

Number of Students

Type of Activity

Learning in Motion • CD-104240